T0370501

HARVEY E. ONE-WOLF

A Visionary's Vision

'Seek and ye shall find'

Isaac Newton's Prophecy about
the End of Days

A Visionary's Vision
Isaac Newton's Prophecy about the End of Days

iUniverse books may be ordered through booksellers or by contacting:

iUniverse
1663 Liberty Drive
Bloomington, IN 47403
www.iuniverse.com
1-800-Authors (1-800-288-4677)

ISBN: 978-1-5320-7966-5 (sc)
ISBN: 978-1-5320-7965-8 (e)

Library of Congress Control Number: 2019911387

Print information available on the last page.

iUniverse rev. date: 08/06/2019

first wild beast
to be slain
&
carcass is burned
in the flame
— Dan 7:11

Spring/S... 2020

#1

Speaking   grandiose   words

THIS MANUSCRIPT COMES

WITH THE USUAL

DISCLAIMER & LIMITATIONS

FOR LIABITY OR REMEDIES

Dan 7:4

A Visionary's Vision

The Newton Prophecy for the Children of Light and the Children of the Day

Harvey E. One-Wolf

Open any modern physics book and you won't have to look far before the name Sir Isaac Newton appears. Isaac Newton was born on Christmas Day (pre-Gregorian calendar) in 1642. He is known for discovering laws of motion, optics, and breaking down white light. He was a philosopher and scholar. He made the first refracting telescope, adding a mirror and a better optical lens. Newton discovered the laws of celestial mechanics and was an avid alchemist. Now we may add biblical prophet to the long list of his remarkable achievements.

Newton was brilliantly minded, possibly autistic, and the epitome of an eccentric genius. At an early age, little Isaac began showing definite signs of emotional disconnection to people. He threatened to murder both his mother and his stepfather, whom he hated, by burning them alive while they slept.

He precociously slipped further into his studies. He saw the world around him with a logical and mathematical eye. No wonder Newton gave the world of science the concept of gravity.

Science is breaking Church rules

Bad boy Newton underground

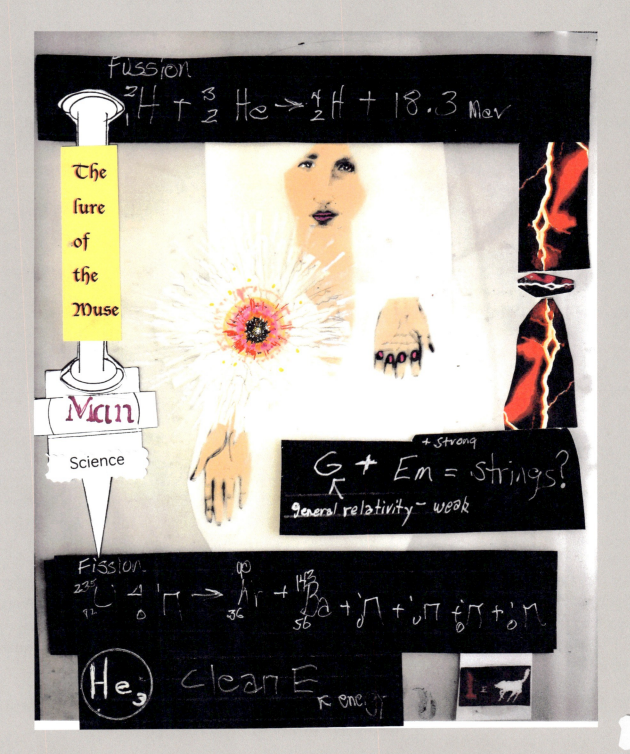

However, he didn't quite have the numbers right. Isaac Newton's formula for gravity was wrong.

It took Albert Einstein (1879–1955) to reformulate the equation. Using his theory of general relativity, Einstein predicted that gravitational waves exist, and his formula was proved correct with the discovery of gravitational waves on February 11, 2016. *G-waves had been directly observed in September 2015 at the Laser Interferometer Gravitational-wave Observatory.   Besides gravity, Isaac Newton applied to the world of mathematics a helm with which to navigate. After Newton, science spoke the language of mathematics evermore. (*Principia Mathematica* was published in 1687 and *Opticks* in 1707.)

Gottfried Wilhelm Leibniz (1646–1716) is credited with co-developing differential calculus. Leibniz was a German philosopher. Independently of Newton, he too invented calculus. He also is credited with coining the term *binary code*, which first appeared in a 1679 article called "*Explication de l'Arthmetique Binaire.*"

Both Newton and Leibniz claimed to be the founding father of calculus, and their arguing became public, creating great anxiety for both.

It should be noted that Albert Einstein used Leibniz's hypothesis that work was proportional to the square of the speed of light—C2, crucial to Einstein's E=mc2.

Engineering science in Newton's day appears to have been more open minded and less biased. The only point at which Newton paid attention to what people thought was when his dis-creditors published claims that refuted his theories and legitimate discoveries.

Isaac Newton sought knowledge and truth from the originator of the universe through the holy scriptures. He believed the universe was designed by a perfect intelligence, rather than being haphazard and arbitrarily contrived, as many finite thinkers believe today.   Modern science turns up hubristic noses at any account of "Creator from beginning to infinite life." God is executing the further development of a constant and precise design, as he has since the founding of the world.

Newton started with a need to know. His desire for spiritual knowledge and belief, which fueled his faith, was equally sought. "The unfolding of God's words are what sheds light. Even the simple will understand" (Psalm 119:30).

The hosts of God are himself and Christ, who is resting and preparing for when his father makes his enemies a footrest while pleading for the holy ones: archangels, cherubs (cherubim), seraphs (seraphim), and angels, who are superior to *Homo sapiens*. Equally superior are the wicked spirit beings, coming from God's own ranks, collectively known as the ubiquitous forces of evil. These beings are active and aggressive—all the more so as each day brings the kingdom of heaven closer. Their agendas are not benevolent, and they favor human extinction.

Newton's three laws of motion :

1st law, to move a body at rest, enough external force must be used to overcome the object's inertia. The larger the object is, the more force is required to move it. ($F = 0$)

2nd law, the force to move a body is equal to its mass times acceleration. ($F = MA$)

3rd law, for every action there is an equal and opposite reaction. ($F_{BC} = -F_{CB}$)

Philosophae Naturalis Principia Mathematica, 1687

The Bringer of Light as an archangel for millennia, the devil has been the ruler of this modern age, whose authority seeks domination to destroy the earth (as deceiver of the nations of the earth), and the air (as spirit beings who aggressively operate in the children of disobedience). Compare Ephesians 2:2–3 NAB.

The Invitation Is Open, but It's Closing Soon

"Taste and see that the Lord Yahweh is good" (Psalm 34:8 NJB).

"The name of Jehovah, is a strong tower. The righteous runneth into him and is safe" (Psalm 18:10 NWT). Harken unto him to live in peace among the chaos, and be quiet to the fear of evil.

"The Lord is nigh to all those who call upon him in truth" (Psalm 145:118–120 KJV). "The Lord watches over all who love him" (NRSV).

"All scripture is by God's inspiration. It is profitable for doctrine, for reproof, for correction, for instruction in righteous" (2 Timothy 3:16 REB).

What true Christians sign up for is offering to be sheep among wolves. Compare Matthew 10:16:

"Be ye therefore as wise as serpents and as harmless as doves" (KJV).

Christians, known as *Christia* in Latin, *Khristianous* in Greek, and *Meshiachiyim* in Hebrew, *Meshianists*, slaves to Christ (Messiah), or *foot followers,* are guides to the Way of Light to those in the darkness and will act as guides through the last tribulation.

Newton's thinking became literal with the experimentation with light, giving us incredible science that has shaped our modern-day world and perhaps the technology yet to come. Newton showed science that white light is not pure. Could Newton have imagined the modern day? He hadn't the imagination to do so. Or did the odd ol' sod?

Sin entered into the world through one man, Adam. Death entered through sin. By Jesus's death comes resurrection of the dead. He is the firstborn of the dead. He also is the ruler of the kings of the earth.

"Do not be afraid of anything you are about to suffer, for the devil will throw some of you into prison for ten days. Remain faithful until death, and I will give you the crown of life" (Revelation 2:10 NAB).

"Whoever wants to save his soul will lose it, but whoever loses his soul for my sake will find it" (Matthew 16:25 NJB).

Jesus himself said, "They will hand you over to be tortured and put you to death" (Matthew 24:9). "The nations will hate you because of my name" (NRSV). "For him they are rendered up as sheep for sacrifice all day long" (Psalm 44:22). "For your sake we have been killed all day long" (Romans 8:36 NWT).

The genealogical race of Abraham, a Hebrew, was originally in Mesopotamia (compare Acts 7:2). Hebrew origins suggested crossing over the river Euphrates, possibly with Abraham, in the area of what is Turkey to Syria today. First mentioned in Genesis 11:3 is Ur of Chaldees, an ancient city on the Euphrates. God promised Abraham that if he moved to a new land, he would bless him, making all the nations of the earth blessed through his seed. By his faith, Abraham was made righteous in

God's eyes (compare Genesis 15:6). Through his seed all the nations of the earth shall be blessed from Abraham down to Jesus down to the Son of Man's next arrival. (Watch for it … coming soon.)

Isaac was the son of Abraham who nearly became a sacred sacrifice to Yahweh. The hand of an angel stopped Abraham from slaying him. God tested the power of Abraham's faith and gave him a grade of A+, which meant he was blessed by God.

Jacob was the son of Isaac, who bought the "right of firstborn to inheritance" from his older twin brother, Esau, for the cost of lentils and meat. An angel with whom Jacob wrestled changed his name to Israel. His twelve sons make up the twelve tribes of Israel.* (See the illustration.)

Jacob, along with his progeny, were treated as royalty during a famine when they were summoned by Joseph, the right hand to the pharaoh of Egypt. Those families proliferated for generations, until the indigenous people feared them. Soon enslavement ensued for the Israelites, and they worked as slaves in Egypt, the iron furnace of the pharaohs.

The God of Abraham, Isaac, and Jacob (Israel) heard their cries. He sent Moses and Aaron before Pharaoh to release these Hebrews. Then the mighty hand of God brought the ten plagues to Egypt until Pharaoh released them.

Moses led the Israelites out of the mighty iron furnace and into the wilderness, guided and instructed by his Almighty God. It is through Moses that God gave the children of Abraham the law.

Jesus fulfilled the law of Moses, making all 613 of them obsolete, but specifically the sacrifice for sin. The law was part of the covenant between Moses, representing the twelve tribes of Israel, and God.

Abram
to
Abraham

Ancestor

Three wandering Armean + Aramaean
Two dying Syrian
One homeless Armean
—Deuteronomy 26:5

Terah, Nachor

Abraham's faith was counted unto him as righteousness.

14 generations to David
David 14 generations to Babylon
Babylon 14 gernerations to Christ

The eternal Almighty promises "By Abram's seed the nations will be blessed."

Abram, son of Terah, later God changes it to Abraham firstborn son: Ishmael from Hagar his wife's handmaid.. Married to Sarai later changed to Sarah (1/2 sister) births:

Isaac + Rebekah (1st cousin) daughter of Betheul the Syrian. births: Esau oldest twin, who sold his birthright for lentils and meat. Jacob younger twin (Israel).

Leah first wife (older Sister and cousins) to Rachel second wife + Zilpah Leah's and Bilhah Rachel's handmaids their progeny make the twelve tribes of Israel:Jacob

Leah (Lackluster)births: Rueben, who loses birthright by laying with Bilhah his father's concubine, slave to Rachel. Simeon (Hearing with acceptance), Levi (adherence joined), Judah (Laudation), Issachar (He brings wages), Zebulun (Habitation).

Bilhah Rachel's handmaid, births: Dan (judge), Naphtali (my wrestling). Becomes property of Rueben.

Zilpah Leah's handmaid births: Gad (good fortune), Asher (hapiness). Rachel (most beloved by Israel) births: Joseph (Increaser),

Benjamin.

Joseph is sold into slavery, where God blesses him and he becomes hand to the Pharaoh of Egypt. All twelve tribes go to Egypt during a great famine. His voice is second only to the pharaoh himself.

Generations later bring Moses and the exodus of the Israelites (Hebrews). Yahweh, Jah Jehovah Gives them Laws and codes to live by down to Christ Jesus. Now the Law lives within the heart and is a spiritual Law.

Became a great and mighty nation. All the nations of the earth shall be Blessed in him. —Gen 18:18

Monad: basic bits of mind. Leibniz believed all matter has them.

Rene Descartes took a philosophical step saying something to the effect of I think, so therefore I am. Gottfried Wilhelm Leibniz told the world of his day, Your mind is all that matters.
Leibniz believed that God is infinite and the holy creator made Monads. Leibniz speculated that the more monads you have the higher your intelligence.

GOTTFRIED WILHELM VON LEIBNIZ   1646–1716
Leibniz, a German philosopher, was a polymath—he was equally at home in abstract studies of logic as he was with mathematics, physics, and philosophy. He invented calculus independently of Newton, and also suggested that an object's ability to do work was proportional to the square of its speed, rather than its speed alone. Squaring an object's speed would become crucial to Einstein's own ideas about $E = mc^2$.

Gottfried Wilhelm von Leibniz

Jesus summed up the first two laws of Moses as the greatest: Love God with your whole heart, soul, and mind, and love your neighbor as yourself (compare Matthew 22:37–40 NAB).

Christians are free from all of the Mosaic laws (compare Acts 15:24 NJB).

Now we are discharged from the Law … Our law is spiritual … so that we are slaves not under the old written code, but in the new life of the spirit (compare Romans 7:6 NRSV).

Jesus gave the world a new code of conduct in kindness and compassion to follow. His sacrifice for the world ended those ancient rituals necessary for good heavenly standing. Rituals of any kind are no longer needed to reach God. Only through the belief that Yahweh answers through the use of Jesus Christ's name as true Christians do we hope in the Lord and wait eagerly for his return.

Peter and the apostles gave no other burdens to the disciples of Jesus besides these: For prosper, brothers, need only refrain from any foods sacrificed to idols, from strangled things, from blood and from fornication (compare Acts 15:20 NWT).

Daniel and John, centuries apart, saw future modern times, including a great dragon, who is the greatest force of evil, a liar and opposer of God. The devil gives to four kings kingdoms, power, and great authority over a nonspecific number of years. The real ruler of this system or world social order, ruling through means of economic, political, and religious deviousness and ultimate control, is Satan.

This system of things is built on two great forces: greed and fear. These forces, which move all the world's markets and drive all the world's trends, are oil based.

Make no mistake: God will bring a government to rule over all the kingdoms of the earth. He will break those kingdoms to pieces, and his kingdom will stand forever (compare Daniel 2:44).

Satan masquerades as the angel of light; likewise agents masquerade as good, but are not (compare 2 Corinthians 11:14–15 NRB).

Lucifer—the devil, an archangel, Dragon and Serpent, and once the Bringer of Light—is a murderer, liar, slanderer, and adversary of the one true God. He is the accuser of our brothers before God (compare Revelation 12:9–10, Proverbs).

Soon the organized religions will lose their control over the governments and nations. Thoughtful and emotional separation of church and state will take place, according to Newton's predictions based on numbers equaling the year 2034.

Dark science and devious and cunning statecraft will be used against honest, good people, who are the true enemies of the coming new world order. Because of God, these awful fascists—four kings from Satan—will add false prophets and lead the doomed, wicked generation straight into the lake that burns with sulfur.

Satan tempted Jesus at the end of his forty-day fast in the wilderness. From a lofty mountain, Satan* showed Jesus all the kingdoms of the earth and told him he would give them to him for one act of worship (a single utterance of praise). The fallen angel of light said, "For that is delivered unto me; and to whomsoever I will give it" (Luke 4:6 KJV).

Jesus answered by quoting the first law Moses was given: love God; him alone shall you worship. The second was to love your neighbor as yourself (compare Luke 4:8 NAB).

The devil is a murderer from the start. No truth is in that one. The lord of darkness is the father of the lie. Jesus told his disciples, "Resist him and he will flee from you."

Satan lied to Eve in the garden of Eden, saying, "Of course you will not die, but rather your eyes will be opened like God's if you eat of the forbidden fruit" (Genesis 3:4 REB).

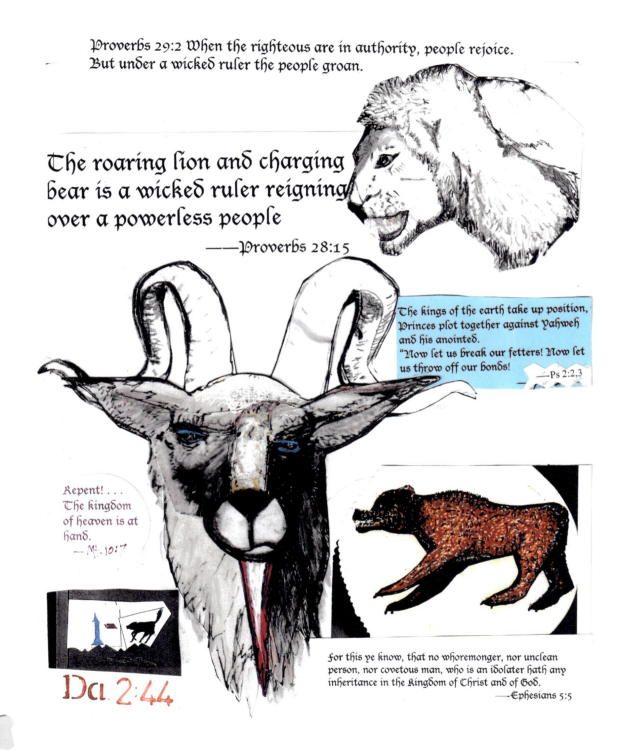

Proverbs 29:2 When the righteous are in authority, people rejoice. But under a wicked ruler the people groan.

The roaring lion and charging bear is a wicked ruler reigning over a powerless people

——Proverbs 28:15

The kings of the earth take up position, Princes plot together against Yahweh and his anointed. "Now let us break our fetters! Now let us throw off our bonds!
—Ps 2:2,3

Repent! . . . The kingdom of heaven is at hand.
— Mt. 10:7

Da. 2:44

for this ye know, that no whoremonger, nor unclean person, nor covetous man, who is an idolater hath any inheritance in the kingdom of Christ and of God.
—Ephesians 5:5

JHVH

Fire	H₂O	Air	Earth

Au

Ag

Cu

Fe

mixed

clay

cut stone

chaff

Ps 35:5
Isa 41:15
Zep 2:2
Mt 3:12

The Revealer of secrets
speaks to Daniel
Nebuchadnezzar first
kingdom the head of Gold.
The last four kingdoms are
the kingdoms of the
Silver rejects.

——Daniel 2:28-44

Wicked are stubble to God . . .
——Isa 47:14
——Mal 4:1

A rebellion took place in heaven. Satan, his gods, and his demons fought against Michael, prince of heaven, an archangel, and the deputized army of heaven. They defeated the dragon, who took a third of the angels out of heaven with him. "No place was found in heaven for him." The dragon, Satan, misleads all of the inhabited earth and all the world's nations, manipulating religions, economics, and politics in a futile attempt to destroy the earth and avoid justice and serving his time in prison (i.e., a thousand-year sentence) (compare Revelation 12:9 NJB). "The devil was hurled down to the earth along with his angels" (Revelation 20:7 NSRV).

Satan's extremely high recidivism rate will last for only a short while next time, causing the second and last death. The dragon is thrown into the lake that burns with sulfur … where the beast and false prophet already are (compare Revelation 20:7).

"Then Death and Hades were thrown into the lake of fire" (Revelation 20:12–15 NRSV), "and anyone whose name was not found written in the book of life was thrown into the lake of fire." "Which means the second death" (Revelation 21:8 NWT).

Alternative Evidence

Newton may have not understood the complexity of the technologies needed to envision the development and uploading of a complex consciousness into "a living soul," but then again, who can? He may not have been able to contemplate the transmutation of a god's consciousness inside a man (Jesus). So Newton accepted a belief in a creator. We must extrapolate that Isaac Newton understood then that the Creator breathed life into *Homo sapiens*. (See the Alchemy Creation illustration.)

Adam was made from the materials every chemistry enthusiast knows: hydrogen, carbon, nitrogen, oxygen, and phosphorous. These elements are commonly found all over the earth. Newton believed this designer and developer of terrestrial human species was the Divine One alone (compare Genesis 2:7). *(*

Daniel 2:20 - 44 says, "*Blessed be the name of God for ever and ever:*
for wisdom and might are his:
He changeth the times and the seasons: he removeth kings,
and setteth up kings: he gives wisdom to the wise, and
knowledge to them that know understanding: He revealeth
the deep secrets things: He knoweth what is in the darkness,
and the light dwelleth with him."

"*And in the days of these kings shall the God of heaven set up*
a kingdom, which shall never be destroyed: and the kingdom
shall not be left to other people, but it shall break in pieces and
consume all these kingdoms, and it shall stand for ever."

Throughout the long echoing corridors of mathematics and science, most people emphatically insist that "humans evolved." Or, "It's natural selection by way of Charles Darwin. End of story!" The evolutionists might hope to reconsider the alternatives that are at play.

Today's scientists have measured only a 7 percent evolution of modern man. Darwin predicated 17 percent in *Origin of Species*. Along with the lack in percentage of evolution since *Homo sapiens* began, scientists are dealing with incomplete data at present. Thus, by definition evolutionists are espousing a "hypothesis of evolution," not a "theory of evolution."

No doubt Charles Robert Darwin (1809–1882), English naturalist, geologist, and biologist, was an extremely intelligent man with an incredible eye for details. But his hypothesis of evolution has flaws in perhaps the same way Newton's formula for gravity was based on known data in his era.

Here is a popular quote by Charles Darwin: "If you had an idea that would outrage society, would you keep it to yourself?"

Darwin, who died in 1882, is buried at Westminster Abbey beneath Sir Isaac Newton's monument.

Some intellectually minded people ask, What are the astronomical odds of unsystematic, random DNA (deoxyribonucleic acid), RNA (ribonucleic acid), and nucleic acids, proteins, lipids, and complex polysaccharides miraculously aligning systemically in a lifeless cesspool of falling minerals? What would be the odds of some haphazard cosmic event spontaneously producing human consciousness in the slime, swimming and crawling through this pool of "perfectly stocked random genes"? This debris puddle of miraculous nonradioactive hydrogen and carbon-based molecules may definitely have produced the "silver rejects" to come.

Great Heros Abound

Francis Crick, biologist and biophysicist (1916–2004), and James Watson, geneticist, zoologist and molecular biologist, showed science the way to the structure of DNA: a double helix polymer of nucleic acid joined by nucleotides, which base pair together.

Newton, of course, would have preferred thinking in terms of human progressive development and the progression of engineering, rather than evolution. Newton didn't know about evolution. His faith allowed for thinking in terms of reverse engineering of God's laws, which govern the universe. Perhaps that explains why Newton uncomfortably said, "Yes, gravity pulls," as many, including well-known scientists who should know better, believe today. The truth is that gravity with space-time is pushing, which Albert Einstein correctly formulated and was proved.

Apart from a miscalculation now and then unbeknownst to him, and despite his apparent contempt for all people in general, iconoclastic Isaac Newton remained an Arian, monotheistic layman practitioner and prodigious reader of the Bible. All that simply means he believed in God and accepted the scriptures as being written through scribes, but the message was personal to him.

The Almighty uses only one intercessor between himself and all humanity: his Son Jesus Christ. Only when you use Jesus's name will he answer your prayer. Newton practiced prayer and abstinence.

Battle plans

7 Seals on the scroll

1st seal "come," says one of the four living creatures (beasts), after the Lamb opened the first seal. An angel riding a White horse is given a crown and bow and arrow. He goes on a quest to conquer.

2nd seal broken by the Lamb, "Come," second living creature said. A red (fiery) colored horse with angel, who is given a sword, to take away peace.

3rd seal opened, third living creature says, "Come." An angel on a black horse is given scales and told to spare the wheat and barley, olive oil and wine.

4th seal is opened "Pale" horse with the forth creature saying, "Death is the angel's name," and "Hades is following." He is given the four acts of judgement. One quarter of the earth he is authorized to kill with his long sword, famine, plagues and wild animals.

5th seal opened and the souls under God's altar grow impatient, but are given white robes and told to wait for their number to be filled.

6th seal causes a great earthquake in heaven. The sun becomes black as sackcloth of hair, Moon turns to blood. Stars fall to the earth like figs in a strong wind. Then heaven is rolled up like a scroll.

7th seal reveals Seven angels is trumpets.

7 trumpets

First trumpet (voices, thunders, lightning, earthquake)= Hail mingled w/ blood, 1/3 of the earth is burned up.

Second angle blows his trumpet. Huge fireball is slammed into the sea, it becomes blood. 1/3 of the sea creatures die. 1/3 boats wrecked.

Third trumpet blast. A great star falls upon the rivers and fountains (Wormwood) Bitterness

Angel number four blows. Sun, Moon and Stars are smitten. 1/3 day 1/3 night

Fifth blast of trumpet. Star falls with the keys to the Pit, Abyss. When it is open smoke raises as if from a massive furnace. **Locusts**, looking like horses in battle gear wearing golden crowns. With men's faces, but women's hair, teeth of lions, with breastplates like iron. Their wings are the sound of a stampede. The tails are like that of scorpions and sting.

They have a King of the Abyss reigns over them. In Hebrew his name is Abandon = destroyer. Greek his name is Apollyon = exterminator.

Sixth angel blows. The angel unties the four angels tied at the Euphrates river. Myriads upon myriads of angels.

Seventh angel happily blasts. The revealed mysteries, sacred secrets are finished. Nations become wrathful God own wrath comes. The Dead from the first resurrection starting beginning of End to End. 1,000 yrs before the rest of Dead are awakened.

Newton would not allow the church to come between himself and God, the Father who sent his Son (Jesus Christ) in the flesh into the world and will send him again soon. According to Newton's prophecy, we have already begun the end of days and are happily waiting for the Son of Man's next trip back to this planet with more God-like qualities and with the holy angels.

Newton himself actually lived, learned, and taught at the prestigious Trinity College of Cambridge University, in England. That is where he read for himself the holy scriptures. He believed throughout some of his long stay at Cambridge that the Father and the Son of Man are two distinctively separate beings. Jesus told his disciples, "If you love me, you would rejoice, I go unto the father, for my father is greater than I" (John 14:28 KJV). Jesus in God form refused to equate himself with the Almighty, but remains his slave … being born in human likeness and being in human form (compare Philippians 2:6 NAB).

The belief in the Trinity sees the Father, Son and Holy Spirit as one God in three divine persons. Newton believed this to be an erroneous Christian doctrine, but he kept his spiritual beliefs to himself, for the most part.

The freedoms that allowed him to do daily activities, which preoccupied him, seemed comfortably easiest to be simply avoided altogether. He felt no need for full disclosure or to experience unavoidable distractions that would undoubtedly have brought him to expulsion.

Newton may have also asked the inspired expression of the prophets, When will the end of days be? Similarly, Peter, Andrew, James, and John asked their teacher (Jesus), When will the end of this age (or system of order or time) be? What will the signs of your return be? Compare Mark 13:3–37.

All anyone knows for sure is that Newton applied logic and mathematics in pursuing a solution to that very problem. What if Newton made predictions only to silence the doomsayers of his time? Whatever motivated him, besides his insatiable hunger for pure knowledge and his thirst for concrete conceptual truth, he based his numbers around the year 800, when Pope Leo III of the Roman Catholic Church made Charlemagne the first Holy Roman Emperor.

King Charlemagne died in 815. Pope Leo III died within a few years of his holy king.

Enter Leo III's confessor Peter Galatin in 1518. This pope introduced the name Jehovah. The covenant name Jehovah of Israel referred to the one true God, standardizing YHWH, a tetragrammaton with no vowels. Through superstition, the Jews stopped pronouncing God's true name aloud and adopted the name Adonai for God.

The church accepted open acts of fornication with kings of the earth (before that, she did her business behind closed doors), fooling at least her faithful, but this open political alignment with the church forced her faithful to turn a blind eye to her lust for power.

Readers should always be cautious: "Only one alone knows," Jesus said, "but about that day and hour, neither the angels in heaven, nor the son, only the Father" (Matthew 24:36 NRSV).

But what if Newton spoke from God? Had he logically worked out the numbers? "Only if

he had been borne along by the holy spirit," said the apostle in 2 Peter 1:21 (NWT).

Regardless, the prophecies of actual times or ages will be examined. You cannot tell by observation when the kingdom of God will come. Jesus told his disciples that it will not happen quickly (compare Luke 17:20 REB).

Har-magedon is the Ancient Greek word for Armageddon (mountain of Megiddo). King Josiah, a beloved king of Judah and Jerusalem, was killed by Pharaoh Nechoh, king of Egypt, in a valley near there. The location is not far from Mount Carmel, in Israel.

The great day of retribution coming to the entire planet will bring punishment to the unrighteous, and substantiation and vindication to the Almighty's name and his faithful people.* All people must be tested. This has figured prominently among the prophets throughout biblical times.

The final place where Satan gathers his armies of the said ten kings of the earth, wild beasts, is at Megiddo, in a last-ditch effort to resist his own apprehension and incarceration for one thousand years in the Tartarus, abyss of densely dark gloom (compare Revelation 20:2).

These disloyal four beasts (kings), silver rejects of the earth, are all stubborn men, who slander about in corruption. They are copper, bronze, lead, and iron … Their dross has not been purged out … "Silver rejects" are what men will call them, and indeed Yahweh has rejected them! "Each is corrupt with too much dross" (compare Jeremiah 6:28–30 NJB).

"Who is the liar, if not the one who claims that Jesus is not the Christ? This is the Antichrist, who denies the Son cannot have the Father either" (1 John 2:22–23 NJB).

What is going to happen when this world order ends? The entire inhabited earth will be under a great trial or test that is to come upon every sentient being. This is a complex tale of the four beasts (silver rejects)—kings, who are the worst of the worst, mentioned in the holy scriptures. These four kings will rise up out of the earth to stand against the Prince of Princes himself (compare Daniel 8:25).

These four wild beasts will be the ones whom John envisioned—John the apostle and son of Zebedee and Salome, brother to James, who wrote John, 1 John, 2 John, 3 John, and Revelation, which took place on the Isle of Patmos. John was exiled for witnessing to Jesus and speaking of God and the composites of wild beasts having qualities of all four beasts, which Daniel had envisioned centuries earlier (compare the prophet Daniel, 604–562 BCE). Daniel was taken into exile by Nebuchadnezzar. Despite his three-year study of pagan occult beliefs, Daniel and his companions remained loyal worshippers of Yahweh.

Shadrach, Meshach, and Abednego faced death by a fiery furnace stoked seven times hotter than usual, but Nebuchadnezzar saw them inside the flames conversing with a figure like the son of gods. The three faithful men survived their death sentence for refusing to bend a knee to the man-made golden statue. Not one hair on them was singed. Daniel was an exiled seer, or prophet, and wrote the book of Daniel. While in exile he served as high priest in Babylon. The ten horns on the seven heads of the first beast, ten diadems, which represent ten kings (ten nations in league of the beast of the earth) hate the great harlot, Babylon the Great (compare Revelation 17:12).

These ten world rulers (kings over principalities) will have one thought from God when they meet with the scarlet-colored beast for one hour: the power and authority to act against the harlot, Babylon, who commits fornication with the kings of the earth and then makes the nations drink the cup of disgusting filth of her sins, driving humanity mad (crazed) with her full cup.

This sorceress (witch, conjurer, fortune-telling mother of all harlots) commits fornication with the kings of the earth, making the people of the world drink the disgusting filth of her acts. She glorifies herself and not God. In her is found the blood of the holy ones (saints, elect, and Jah's people) and of all the prophets, and all those who have died (slaughtered by the sword). This sorceress—witch and spiritual practitioner of sin, divination, and wickedness—is in league with the ruler of this age. She has been deceived by Satan while misdirecting the nations.

Her sentence is death by fire and fury. Newton predicted that this will occur in 2034.

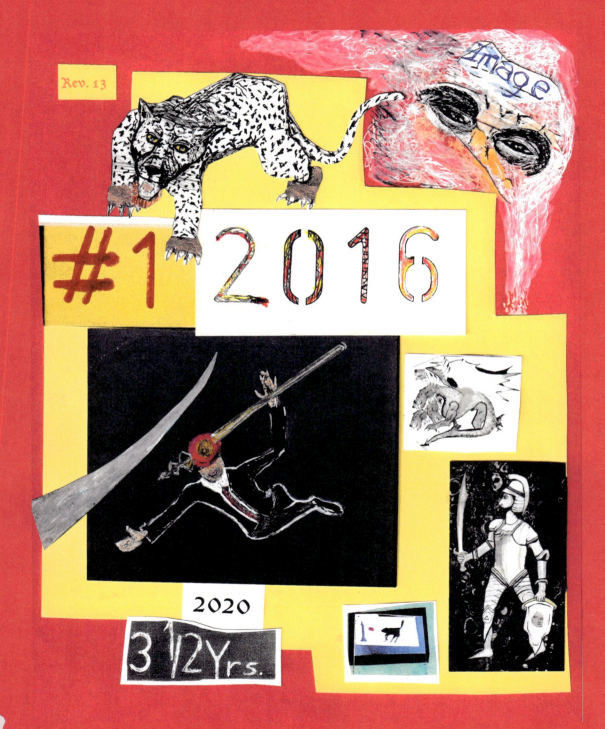

10:16

31

The Sorceress Who Refuses to Repent

Fallen, fallen, Babylon the Great became a dwelling place for demons and a haunt for every unclean spirit and foul bird. The merchants have grown rich by your shameless luxuries, extravagant riches, and drive for power (compare Revelation 18:2–3). "In Babylon the Great is found guilt for the blood of all prophets and saints, and all who have been slaughtered upon the earth" (Revelation 18:24 NAB).

The Divine Oneself, the Amen, has become king. Hallelujah (alleluia) and praise Jah, you people. Let the coastlands and Islands rejoice (compare Psalm 97:1).

The heavenly concierge angel rebuking John for kneeling to worship him warned, Be careful, I am a fellow slave of you and your brothers who have the work of witnessing to Jesus. God alone you must worship … For the bearing witness to Jesus is what inspires prophesying (compare Revelation 19:10 NWT). Blessed are those have been called to the wedding feast of

the Lamb (compare Revelation 19:9 NAB).

The foreordained promise is that the true believers shall be considered for divine protection from the predicted wrath or a resurrection to everlasting life. I will never again curse the ground because of humankind, nor will I ever again destroy every living creature as I have done with the flood (compare Genesis 8:21 NRSV).

The other important foreordained promise is that none who put faith in the Lord will be disappointed. "For everyone who calls on the name Jehovah will be saved" (Romans 10:13 NWT). It is the one who is righteous who will live by faith (compare Romans 1:16–17 NRSV).

"Any destined for captivity goes into captivity, any destined to be slain by the sword shall be slain by the sword" (Revelation 13:10 NAB).

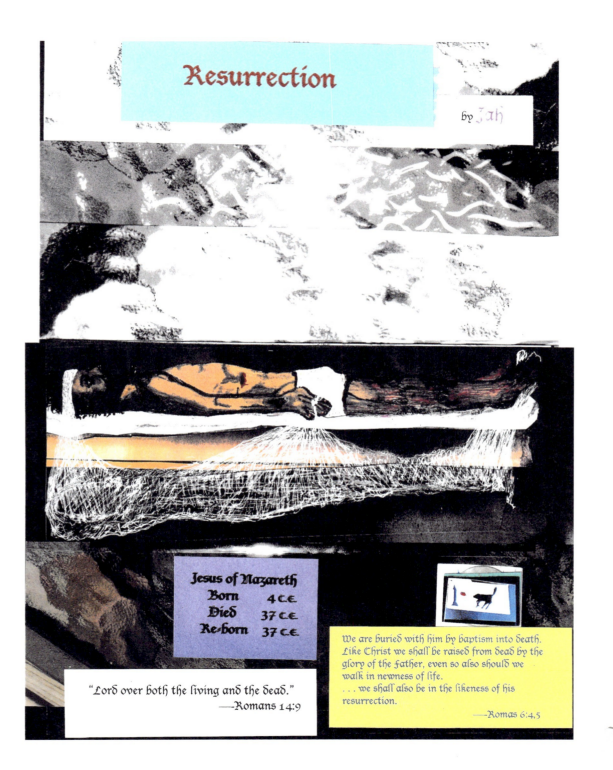

Resurrection

by Jah

Jesus of Nazareth
Born   4 C.E.
Died   37 C.E.
Re-born   37 C.E.

"Lord over both the living and the dead."
—Romans 14:9

We are buried with him by baptism into death.
Like Christ we shall be raised from dead by the
glory of the Father, even so also should we
walk in newness of life.
. . . we shall also be in the likeness of his
resurrection.

—Romas 6:4,5

Children of light and children of the day, show patience. Show patience! ... "The light of the righteous rejoices, burns brightly; the lamp of the wicked will be extinguished" (Proverbs 13:9 REB). Let the unrighteous practice unrighteousness still ... Let the holy pristine be pristinely holy still. The curse shall be lifted. "The throne of God and of the Lamb shall be in it" (Revelation 22:3 KJV). They said to the spiritually thirsty, Lo, drink of waters of life. It will be yours to drink freely (compare Isaiah 55:1, John 7:37, Revelation 7:17, 21:6, 22:17).

God's references to the "children of light and the children of the day" are found in Ephesians 5:8 and 1 Thessalonians 5:5.

The one full of grace, mercies, and tenderness—our God—will be there in the precise moment to save his faithful, steadfast believers (compare Psalm 116:5).

The light from God will shine on you and light your way, if only you will repent. Mountains will totter and hills shake, but the promise of God's love will remain with you. "My steadfast love shall not depart from you" Isaiah 54:10 (NRSV). Blessed are those who die in the Lord from hereafter until the end of this world order. The good deeds go right with the upright when they die (compare Revelation 14:13).

The wild beast ascends out of the sea (see illustration) with seven heads, upon its ten horns having ten diadems (coronets), and blasphemous names (compare Revelation 13:1–2).

The first silver reject, who crawled out of the sea, is like a lion and has the wings of an eagle. The wild beast's wings will be plucked out of it, so it is made to stand with two legs upon the earth like a man. The first silver reject is given a heart and human mind (compare Daniel 7:4 NRSV).

The second silver reject extremely endorses the first silver reject. The second silver reject will make those of the earth worship the first silver reject's image, whose mortal wound (death stroke or sword stroke) will be healed to one of its seven heads (compare Revelation 13:14). The beast was allowed to mouth its boasts and blasphemies ... The first silver reject will lose its kingdom after only forty-two months (compare Revelation 13:5).

The first silver reject will eventually die (compare Daniel 7:11). Then a lengthening of life will be given to the second and third silver rejects, "for an appointed time and a season" (Daniel 7:12 REB). But no longer will numbers two and three rule over a kingdom. They retain great authority and will wield great power and much influence behind the scenes with all conspirators of darkness.

Worldwide, people admire the first silver reject's image. Followers even genuflect before the dragon, giving Satan thanks for giving them this wild beast. They worship the beast, cheering, Who is like him? Who can battle him? (Compare Revelation 13:4.)

Here God sternly warns, Whoever worships the beast, images or receives the mark, #666, the number of their name, not one of these is written in the Lamb's Book of Life (compare Revelation 13:8).

The image of the wild beast will both speak and cause those to be killed who do not worship its image (compare Revelation 13:15).

The second silver reject, having two small horns like a lamb's but speaking like a dragon, comes in like a bear. Its claws are like copper. It will have witnessed the false prophet's making fire (lightning or weaponry) come down from heaven (compare Revelation 13:11–13). This false prophet will promise great new energies, wealth, prosperity and economic ideas, and peace and security to help usher in a new era for a brave new world.

The number 666 will be received in the right hand or forehead to buy or sell. Noncompliance will not be lawfully acceptable (compare Revelation 13:13–16). This will be introduced by the false prophet and the second silver reject. Certainly, identity theft will no longer happen, but the order is clear: do not accept the number of the name of the first silver reject or worship its image.

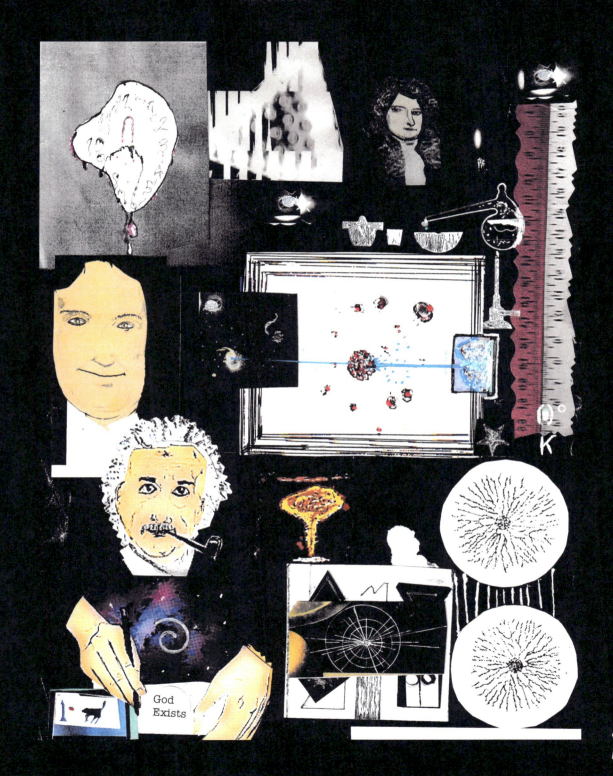

God Exists

Great darkness	First Light	Waters separating

Elements in chaos	Sun imposed order	God beginning creation

Dodging logic, numbers mix like the letters that scramble.
Teachers and principals quickly discard. An academic
dumpster-child of sorts. Until I was turned out.
God stopped the letters inverting themselves once my
twenties rolled around. Go to now.
My vision is clear, my heart is true and my art finite-fixed
until the end.
Under the aegis of the Ancient of Days, may our work be a
spark that ignites the fuse, which shall burn down the
Devil's arsenal

Harvey E. One-Wolf

So begins the unpleasant endurance test of God's people. Take courage and throw your burdens on he who lives forever and ever. Let your heart be with love of God and not with love of money.

The new progression will be for economics, superior technologies, and highly advanced weaponry, which comes with the second silver reject, who will witness the false prophet's skills firsthand. The second silver reject comes with three ribs between its teeth, it being like a bear. They (ungodly and wicked ones) will shout at the beast, 'Get up and eat up much flesh! … '" But after destroying Babylon the Great, its power and kingdom doesn't last long (compare Daniel 7:5).

Then comes the third beast, the third silver reject. It is like a leopard with four wings of a flying creature on its back and four heads. The third silver reject seems inert. What appeared next seemed to alarm and frighten the prophet Daniel. The fourth beast, the fourth silver reject, is mightier and more cunning than the first three silver rejects before it. This one is larger than its fellows.

This last silver reject is highly intelligent and successful, yet treats women most disrespectfully and embarrasses the three before it. This dictator does as he pleases and is richer than all before him. With its boastful mouth it blasphemes, but it has great charm and intelligence too, and unlimited influence, and puts on great airs. Its kingdom will be broken and divided into the four winds of the earth when it stands up (takes power) (compare Daniel 11:4).

In a wonderful way it will cause devastation to many. The fourth silver reject will bring mighty princes down and important ones, and also the holy ones (compare Daniel 8:23–25). The fourth silver reject will tread down with its feet and wage war with the holy one of the earth. It will gather the already mentioned infamous ten armies of the earth to do battle against the Lamb and his heavenly angelic army.

Newton prophesied that Armageddon—Megiddo—will take place in 2060. His final words on this matter were a grumbling, "Only the people in that age will know."

According to Newton's calculations, God will specifically burn Babylon the great (the Roman Catholic Church) completely through the scarlet-colored wild beast (compare Revelation 17:1–18) in 2034.

"Leave her, my people, let each one save himself from the burning wrath of the Lord" (Jeremiah 51:45 NAB).

Babylon the Great is an empire of many false religions. When the daughter of Babel, Jezebel, who calls herself a prophetess, does fall, "In one day her judgements, retributions, and plagues will cause mourning, famine and death. She will be completely burned with fire which unknowingly carries out God's planted idea.

All Must Choose a Master

Whenever Babylon goes down, this will signal that the Almighty is beginning his reign as king. "God will be the Supreme Judge presiding and examining his created earth" (Revelation 19:6 NWT). "Guilty," he will say as the verdict in his court. "Innocent are the holy ones."

The supreme judge has given Babylon centuries to repent, but she refuses to repent of her fornication and her murders. "I sit a queen and I am no widow and shall see no sorrow." In that is why her plagues come instantly upon her (Revelation 18:7 KJV).

The Most High telling the finale from the beginning.

The covenant is Peace.

The promise is everlasting life, rest, with God's love never leaving us.

The Commandents:
Love God with all of your heart;
Love thy neighbor as thyself.

The two anointed

Revelation 11: 3

Psalms 18:2;
Psalms 71:3

Jer 23:23

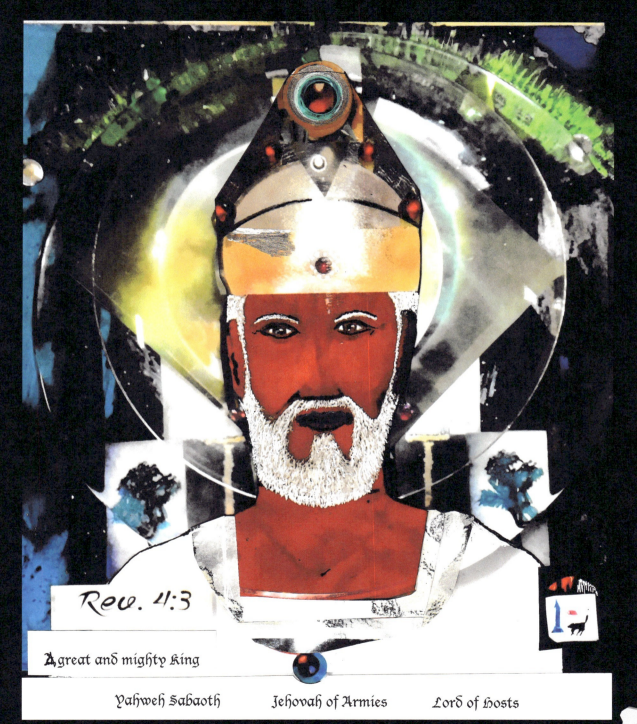

Rev. 4:3

A great and mighty king

Yahweh Sabaoth   Jehovah of Armies   Lord of Hosts

Yet repented not of the works of their hands, that they should not worship devils, idols of gold, silver, bronze, stone and wood, which neither see, nor hear, nor walk. Neither repented they of their murders, nor sorceries, nor fornication, nor their thefts (compare Revelation 9:20–21).

God himself wondered, What agreement does the temple of God have with idols? … We are temples of our living God (compare 2 Corinthians 6:16, 18 NRSV). Touch nothing unclean and I will welcome you … I will be your Father and you will be my sons and daughters. It is the righteous and blameless who follow the footsteps of the good and keep on the narrow path. It is the righteous who will live in the land. The upright and blameless ones are those who survive. They, who are the leftovers after the greatest tribulation, shall live securely on the earth. But as for the wicked they shall be cut off of the land (compare Proverbs 2:20–22).

"Put not your trust in princes, nor in any son of man in whom there is no help. His breath goes forth, he returns to his earth; in that very day his thoughts perish" (Psalm 146: 3–4 KJV).

These four silver rejects choose to battle for the devil, for they are sons of Satan. They all are like he-goats to those from heaven. How the beings of heaven must laugh at them.

What especially sets these four silver rejects apart from acclaimed megalomaniac psychopaths like Hitler, Stalin, Saddam Hussein, or any other despot is that these bully autocrats are given seats of power, kingdoms, and great authority by Satan (compare Revelation 13:1–18).

These awful, four silver rejects, as God called them, will destroy the earth in God's sight.

Isaiah's prophetic vision saw "the very land polluted under inhabitants themselves for bypassing the laws, and statutes and the ancient covenant" (Isaiah 24:5–6 NWT). "That is why a curse devours the earth." The earth will pale in the predicted coming of the great tribulation, which will be so violent and full of lawlessness, no flesh should survive. For the safety of the holy ones, God cuts short those days (compare Matthew 24:21–22).

worship

prophet

Murderer,   Liar,   Traitor,
Great knowledge of sin and sorrow.
Destruction and misery are his ways.
No fear of God before his eyes.
His offer freedom from conscience.

the Devil

ROUTE
666

The Devil giving power to the false prophet, who misleads all the world.

Resist him.

Jah, protect me, in Jesus' name.

Revelation 13:1-18

45

Newton had many colleagues—intellectuals—believing this in his day. The year the first silver reject is to appear, Newton prophesied, would be 2016. The first silver reject will be washed up out of the sea of humanity. To God the wicked are a sea in turmoil, washing ashore seaweed, filth, and mire. The first wild beast stood like a leopard, but had the feet of a bear and the mouth of a lion. The dragon gave him power, his seat, with great authority (compare Revelation 1, 2).

That generation will not pass away until these things take place, Jesus foretold. Newton claimed centuries ago that the twenty-first century will see the coming of the end times, which is the end of man's reign over the earth.

The last days will be critical, terrifying, desperate times. People will be self-centered and lovers of money, heartless, hedonistic, inflexible, boastful, and blasphemous. They will have a form of godly devotion but stand false to its power; from these people turn away (compare 2 Timothy 3:1–4).

Skeptics need only look at the truth around them to see that the wheels and gears are turning and the body is set into motion. (See Newton's law of motion.) Make no mistake: these signal the end of man's world order. Who can stop it? Who can stand up against the dragon? The easy answer is He who was, who is, and who is coming. Take comfort from the good news of our coming Lord, bringing a new way for children of light and children of the day.

Have patience, pray, and stand upright. Find comfort in his word for yourself. Do not put your spiritual life in the hands of any child of Adam. We are to be judged individually. Call upon him who lives for infinity for directions, and follow them.

This is how to tell who are God's children and who are the devil's: anyone who fails to do what is right or love his fellow-Christian is not a child of God (compare 1 John 3:10 REB).

"For not the one who recommends themselves is approved, but the one whom God recommends."

Acts 4:13

II Corinthians 10:18

"Honor among you, love for the brothers and sisters in faith, and have honor for the king."—I Peter 2:17

"Thou shalt not revile the gods, God, nor curse the ruler of thy people."—Exodus 23:28

"I am against you, O ruinous mountain," Jehovah says. "You destroyer of the entire earth. I will stretch out my hand and roll you away from the crags and make you a burned out mountain."—Jeremiah 51: 25

ヨ 7 ヨ 7

The evil Dragon
swims in
the south pacific,
His throne is in
Jerusalem.
But the Eternal Almighty
will reclaim his Mt. Zion
soon.
Let the day of the East wind come.

Mark A. Harvey

Harvey One-Wolf

The fourth silver reject, who is terribly terrible and exceptionally strong, will have no one to come to his aid while militarily camping between the grand sea and the holy Land of Decoration. The four silver reject comes to its end. He has had a time, time and half a time to crush the power and happiness of the holy ones (compare Daniel 12:7).

Silver rejects two and three, including the false prophet, will be pitched alive into the fiery lake of burning sulfur. As for the rest, they will be killed by the sword protruding before the mouth of the Son of Man (compare Revelation 19:19–21).

The Son is in his Father's glory, being he is a god and will not be returning in man's image. Do not look for false Christs or prophets among men (compare Matthew 24:26).

Then said he, … For just as lightning strikes from one end of heaven to the other, from one end of earth to the other, so will the Son of Man be on that Day (compare Luke 17:24–30).

Jesus told us, Just as on the day of Lot leaving Sodom it rained sulfur, brimstone, and fire and destroyed all of them. So will it be also on the day the Son of Man is revealed.

For those who know their God, the fourth silver reject plants the image that will cause desolation in the holy place. Before he sleeps in death, this king of the wild beasts worships, giving glory to a graven image (a god of fortresses or strongholds). Desolation, appalling abomination, is put up in the holy place Daniel spoke of (compare Matthew 24:15).

The fourth silver reject places the appalling sight of desolation, which causes amazement and disgust, where the normal seals (reverence place) should go. This alien god their fathers haven't heard of before, nor their grandfathers (compare Daniel 11:24–31).

There will be an account of 1,290 days until number four's end … Happy are those in expectations and for those who arrive at the 1,335th day (compare Daniel 12:12).

The seventh angel pours his bowl into the "air," spiritual and higher beings are apprehended and dealt with by deputized higher beings, and a righteous judge sentences them (compare Revelation 16:17–18, 20:1–3).

"Babylon was a golden Cup in Yahweh's (Jehovah's and the Lord's) hand. She made all the nations of the whole earth drunk (drunk of her wine) and because of this they have become mad (crazed)."——Jeremiah 51:7

"Depart (get out and come out) of her my people if you do not want to share with her in the sins (crimes) and receive a share in her plagues."——Revelation 18:4

Yahweh (Jehovah), Lord God is King. Give him glory.
Hallelujah, Alleluia, Praise Jah, you people.
Happily blessed are those invited to the marriage banquet of the Lamb.
His bride is adorned with shiningly clean, bright fine linen.
(linen signifies the righteous acts of God's people)——*Revelation 19:1-9*

Jesus said the sun will grow dark, the moon will not give light, and the stars will fall from heaven and the powers of heaven will be shaken (compare Matthew 24:29). A great earthquake such as has not happened before the forming of earth occurs. (compare Revelation 16:18, Hebrews 12:26, Ha. 2:6).

Then a great hail occurs. "With every stone weight of a talent = 33–50kg (75–110 lbs.) will fall upon the wicked and ungodly people. They die cursing the One who made the plague (compare Revelation 16:21).

With a loud noise or hissing sound the sky (heaven) dissolves, the world is discovered, and all that is in the earth is brought to judgment. The sacred secret, which God declared to his own slaves and the prophets, is brought to finish. "Look, I am making all things new," says the One seated on the throne (compare Revelation 21:5).

The heaven and earth melt with elements of fire and the destruction of the ungodly ones. Heaven dissolves and the earth is full of discoveries. Full disclosure: once heaven itself rolls up like a scroll, God's examination of his creation will begin.

According to the promises, a new heaven and new earth await where righteousness dwells (compare 2 Peter 3:7–13). God will give permission to eat from the tree of life that is in the paradise garden of God (NRSV). To any who are victorious and conquer, they will taste the fruit of life's tree (compare Revelation 2:7).

Victory and conquering is over the wild beast, his image, and his number.

Whoever conquers will eat hidden manna and be given a white pebble with their new name inscribed, which only those receiving know. Compare Revelation 2:17. Manna is food for angels. Who conquers will be arrayed in white outer garments. I will not strike his name from the Book of Life. I will acknowledge their name before my Father and his angels (also as belonging to Christ). Compare Revelation 2:5.

"To the conqueror, I will grant to sit down at my throne" (Revelation 3:21 NWT). To rule with Christ for a thousand years before turning the earth over to his Father, be among the holy 144,000. The elect, holy ones, saints spots are still be open.

All true Christians are reproofed and disciplined by the Father. "Lo, my Father will finish your training," Jesus said to anyone who is to be a disciple. He has affection for you the way a father has for his son (compare Proverbs 3:12). God disciplines his children (compare Revelation 3:19). As many as God loves, he rebukes and chastens with scourges (reproves and trains). Be zealous and repent in earnest.

Come As You Are

Truth may change reprobate minds and ones who have impenitent hearts, and may overturn deeply rooted things. Whoever heeds his words and trusts in Him who sent Jesus forth has eternal life. Jesus tells us: Lo, whoever listens to my words, and believes in the one who sent me has eternal life; without being brought to judgment such a persons passed from death to life (John 5:24 NJB).

God doesn't want your money, because he owns all the gold and silver in the mountains and in the heavens. He doesn't want your sacrifices or tithings, despite what is otherwise spoken in the organized religions. God wants your mercies and compassion for other people and acts of kindness. Loving God means you follow his rules. Despite knowing that, sometimes it is hard to simply be nice. Who shouldn't try to forgive others so that they may be forgiven? God wants repentance and the invocation of his spirit into your life. God wants into your heart.

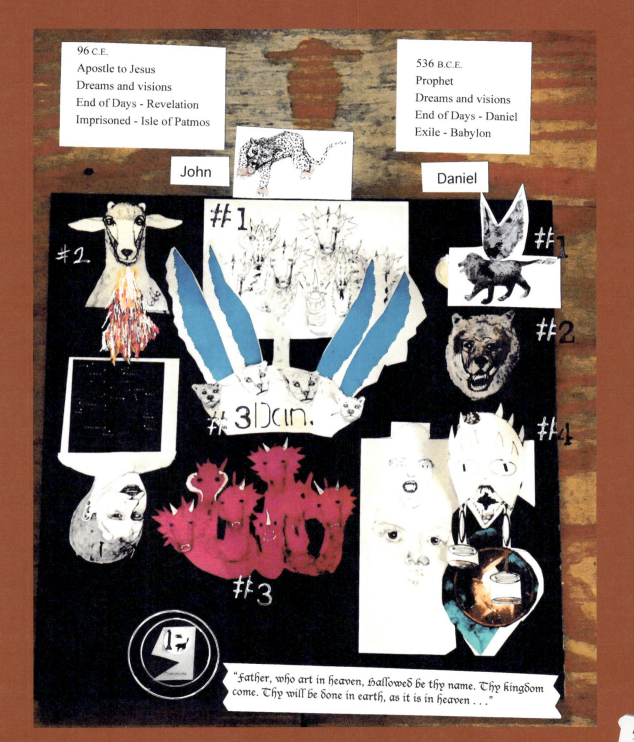

Save yourselves, Peter wrote, when asked how to proceed: repent and get baptized and be forgiven of your sins and then receive the Holy Spirit from God. God takes no delight in the destruction of anyone, but "my Lord God" is patient and wants all peoples, nations, and tongues to come to repentance (compare 2 Peter 3:9). "God is long-suffering to us, not willing that any should perish, but that all should come to repentance" (KJV).

"The love of God means that we observe his commandments: and yet they are not burdensome" (1 John 5:3 NAB). His laws he writes in our hearts and minds.

God shall pass the one-third who survive the fire. He shall refine them as silver is refined, and test them as gold is tested. Yahweh Sabaoth says two-thirds in it will be cut off (killed) and the other third will be left. He shall pass this third through the fire … Refine them as silver is refined" (compare Zechariah 13:9 NJB).

The foreordained warning is this: Do not allow anything between you and Yahweh, Jehovah, Lord. Invoke the name of Jesus Christ the Son. Believe that God the Father will save you, and he will. But then do praise him and prove yourselves faithful and endure the ten days (on water and vegetables, like Daniel and his companions) in your prison or unto death if necessary, and eternal life is yours. Or fall short to an eternal second death in the lake of burning sulfur.

Put on the whole armor of God … our struggle is not against enemies of flesh and blood, but against rulers, against authorities, against the Cosmic powers of this present darkness, against the spiritual forces of evil in heavenly places (compare Ephesians 6:11–17 NRSV).

Sir Isaac Newton believed in science and God. The existence of one inside his mind did not threaten the other. Rather, it opened a door of perception in him so he could gain advanced knowledge of how God's universe is designed and operating. "If I have seen further," Sir Isaac Newton said, "it is because I have stood on the shoulders of giants."

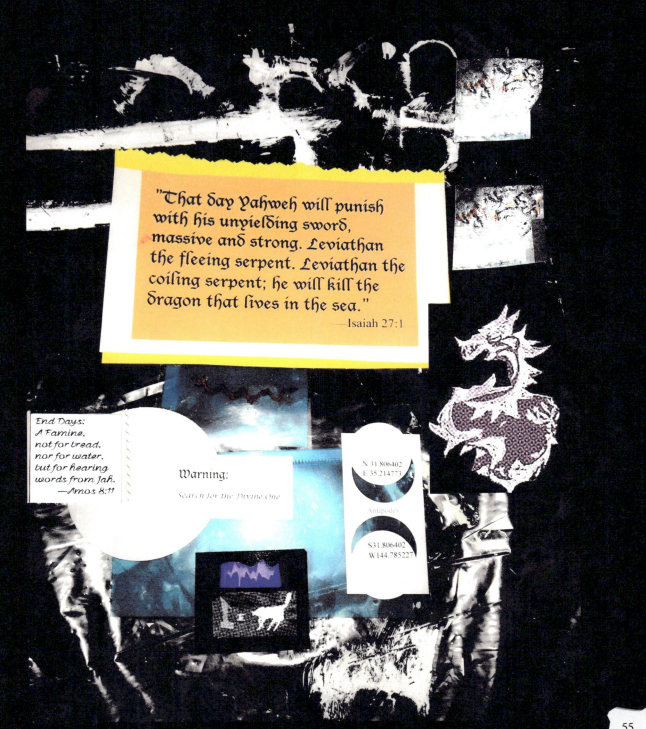

"That day Yahweh will punish with his unyielding sword, massive and strong. Leviathan the fleeing serpent. Leviathan the coiling serpent; he will kill the dragon that lives in the sea."

—Isaiah 27:1

End Days:
A Famine,
not for bread,
nor for water,
but for hearing
words from Jah.
—Amos 8:11

Warning:

Search for the Divine One

N 31.806402
E 35.214773

Antipodes

S 31.806402
W 144.785227

Whether Newton's prophecy numbers prove inaccurate or not, his work of discoveries lives on, until the last day, at least. How many of Newton's accomplishments will survive Jesus's own prophecy? … Is it truly an angel's measure as man? … or an angel using man's math? … That's highly unlikely. Advanced math has always come from gods or the Akashic record through those who were open to it.

Be forewarned again: if Newton's numbers are flawed, the end of days might come sooner than expected. Do not rely upon Newton's known data. Use your general relativity to prepare for full-dimensional life in the Way. Read the Bible for yourself and pray. Listen to God and do as he tells you.

Watch and stay awake, for you do not know when your Lord is coming. I tell you, be on watch, stay alert. "Keep looking, keep awake for you do not know when the appointed time is" (Mark 13:35–37 NWT).

You may have to act quickly. Be ready and watchful, all who hope in the good news of God's coming kingdom. The Holy City will be trampled on by many nations, and God's two witnesses will shut the sky from raining for 1,260 days while prophesying. The two witnesses will be dressed in sackcloth and have the abilities to cause water to turn to blood and strike the earth with any plague they wish.

The two witnesses will be conquered and killed. The world will rejoice, and send presents. Many demons like the sending around of presents. But after lying unentombed and decomposing for several days and half in the Broadway, life from the Almighty is sent back into them, reanimating the two witnesses to full consciousness. They ascend to heaven in a cloud. Within fleeting moments to an hour, the great earthquake occurs and one-tenth of the city falls, killing seven thousand people. The seventh trumpeter angel sounds his instrument. The sacred secret has come to a finish. Sovereignty over the world has passed to our Lord and his Christ, and he shall reign forever (compare Revelation 11:15–16 REB).

But the nations become wrathful. Then wrath from God comes. The Almighty's wrath destroys them, and judgments of the dead take place. Some people experience a resurrection to eternal life, but some experience a judgment of being cut off, or complete destruction.

But woe to the fearful, and the unbelieving, and the abominable, and murderers, and whoremongers, and sorcerers, and idolaters, and all of the liars shall have their part in the lake which burns with fire and brimstone: which is the second death (Revelation 21:8 KJV).

Remember, it is through persecutions, tribulation, and hardships that we enter into the kingdom of God (compare Acts 14:22).

Believe, for any who believes in the Son of Man and Father in heaven will have eternal life. Any refusing to believe or obey God's retribution must be endured (compare John 3:36).

If within forty-two months a king steps down because of being unable to continue, the countdown to the end of ages will have begun. If Newton's prophecy is in motion, the course of correct mathematical prediction remains to be proved. Do repent and worship God, turn away from Satan's authority, and do works fit for repentance. "The good news of the kingdom will be proclaimed through the world, as a testimony to all the nations: and then the end will come" (Matthew 24:14 VRSV).

May the light from God beam forth a stream out of his right hand, for he holds two rays. One ray beams forth a stream of righteousness, hope, joy, peace, and holy spirit into the hearts of the children of the light and the children of the day. The other ray is the grand owner's concealed might (compare Habakkuk 3:4 NWT).

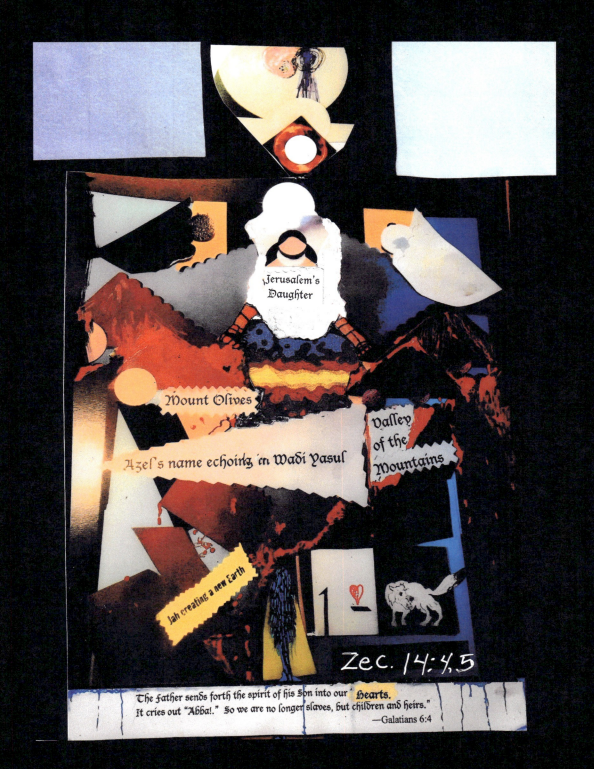

In the spirit of Jesus, one must be humble, gracious, generous, and loyal to be called God's true child, called by the sharp sword of truth (compare Acts 16:7).

I will tell you a mystery (sacred secret): "flesh and blood can never possess the kingdom of God. We shall not all die, but we shall all be changed" (1 Corinthians 15:50–51 REB).

The survivors will be taken up in the air to meet our Lord. "Then we which are alive and remain shall be caught up together with them in the clouds, to meet the Lord in the air" (1 Thessalonians 4:17 KJV). Be watchful, and hope in the good news of our Morning Star.

Final words on a great visionary: Sir Isaac Newton understood the promise that Jesus himself promised us, which is life everlasting. Perhaps one day soon, God willing, we may all meet.

Life is a leap of faith. Believe, do good works, and call on the Sovereign himself in his Christ's name.

Sodom's error was her pride. She grew haughty and too well fed, carefree from having been kept undisturbed. The hand of the afflicted and poor she did not aid.

Sodom

Oholah

Samaria

Oholibah

Jerusalem

Jerusalem's disgusting acts are worse than those of her sisters Samaria and Sodom.
Her deeds by comparison make her sisters both righteous.
Jah-Jehovah removed them from before his sight and He shall remove you as well.

References

Bibles used for reference on all scripture compared and quoted:

New American Bible (NAB). 1991. Confraternity of Christian Doctrine.

New Jerusalem Bible (NJB). 1985. Darton, Longman & Todd and Doubleday.

New Revised Standard Version (NRSV). 1989. Division of Christian Education of the National Council of the Churches of Christ in the United States of America.

New World Translation of the Holy Scriptures (NWT). 1984. Watch Tower Bible and Tract Society of New York.

Revised English Bible (REB). 1989. Oxford University Press and Cambridge University Press.

King James Version (KJV). 1970. Thomas Nelson.

Boyd, Robert, and Joan B. Silk. 2003. *How Humans Evolved.* W. W. Norton.

Freedman, Roger A., and William J. Kaufmann III. 2002. *Universe.* W. *H. Freedman.*

Halliday-Resnick-Walker. 2005. *Fundaments of Physics.* John Wiley and Sons.

Kirkpatrick and Wheeler. 1993. *Physics: A World View.* Saunders College Publishing.

The New Compact Bible Dictionary. 1967. Zondervan.

PBS. *Nova.* "Einstein's Big Idea." Aired October 11, 2005. Promotional poster.

Rooney, Anne. 2015. *The Story of Physics.* Arcturus.

The World Book Encyclopedia of Science (Physics Today). 1985. World Book.

Science and Technology Dept., Carnegie Library of Pittsburgh. 1994. *The Handy Science Answer Book.*

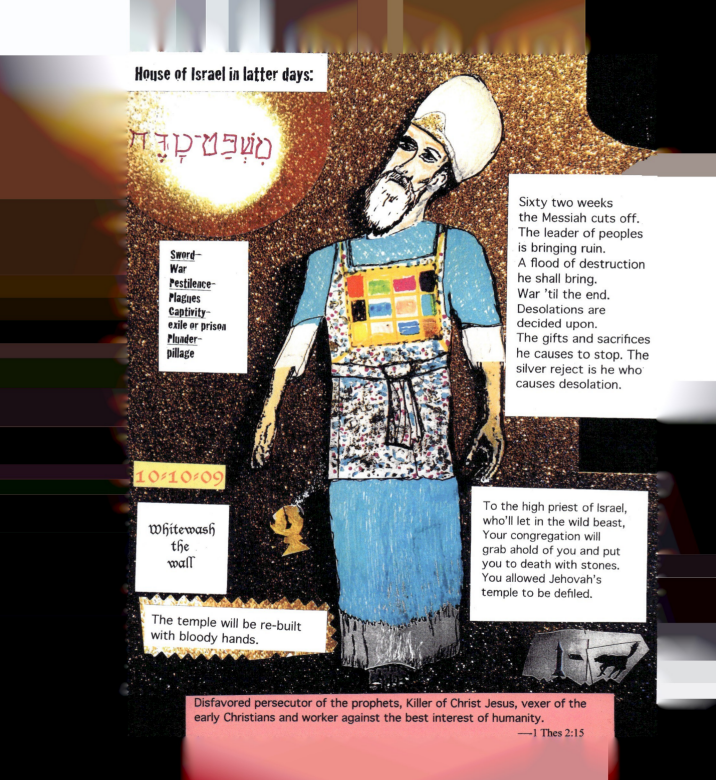

House of Israel in latter days:

מְשֻׁמֵּד

Sword—
War
Pestilence—
Plagues
Captivity—
exile or prison
Plunder—
pillage

Sixty two weeks
the Messiah cuts off.
The leader of peoples
is bringing ruin.
A flood of destruction
he shall bring.
War 'til the end.
Desolations are
decided upon.
The gifts and sacrifices
he causes to stop. The
silver reject is he who
causes desolation.

10·10·09

Whitewash
the
wall

The temple will be re-built
with bloody hands.

To the high priest of Israel,
who'll let in the wild beast,
Your congregation will
grab ahold of you and put
you to death with stones.
You allowed Jehovah's
temple to be defiled.

Disfavored persecutor of the prophets, Killer of Christ Jesus, vexer of the
early Christians and worker against the best interest of humanity.
—1 Thes 2:15

About the author:

A scribbler, a scratcher, a clay vessel of His unmerited mercies. Self-described as "a writer with serious art therapy issues, trying to remember pleasant words are as a honeycomb, sweet to the soul and health to bones, while awaiting the terrible day. Wanting events to rapidly progress, but knowing the Almighty is in control."

Look for the publication of Harvey E. One-Wolf's science-fiction work:

How to Condense Your Universal Consciousness
Small Enough to Survive Cygnus X*1 or (9*Xr's)

A special thanks to A. Merizon for her editorial gifts, and for going lightly on me.
Thank you, my beloved Shady Gray, for being my soul's inspiration.
And to Tony, Jordan, Alisha and Andrew.
I praise Jah, my muse.

To prosper, love the Almighty with all of your heart, soul, and being.
Pray in Christ Jesus's name. Yeshua, son of the Most High God. Christ King above all nations.

Son of Destruction

bad news

#4

Extreme intelligence and lack of empathy have earned great wealth, power and authority. How sweet the taste. $$$ Greed/Fear you lust for

But you contend with God himself. He has no right, says the wicked one who gathers what does not belong to him. crook Fraud blood

You see the ways of your enemies. You sneer at their fortified strongholds. Their riches for plunger wait. spoils of WAR

Your eagle flies in the wake of your alien-god. Pleiades? Satan fell out of Orion.

Either way they are going to the same Tartarus, Abyss of dense gloom of incarceration.

Your assemblies of violence are faces of the east wind.

The sweetness goes out of your mouth.

Jah-Jehovah and his Christ Jesus are in place. Let their kingdom come. Father & son

You were deceived. You are in a net your cannot get out of.

Rage to destroy without mercy, for the reports are not right.

Synchronization all out of sorts.

Remember to tell your assassin that you are a god.

Your god, nor anyone is able to save you on this night. The statue and the Image lay dead on the ground. When Jah thunders out of heaven, in turmoil

As for your assassin, he'll hide away in his little nation, until he too soon dies, amounting to nothing. The same as you. Your Army turns on itself!....

All of your possessions will be pillage for the survivors.

Your Honor is turned into Dishonor. Their Slaughter

The others know time is almost up. Counter nothing much. #2 #3

The coming kingdom has come. is great. 11 Nation Army

Soon a speedy riddance to all the wicked. and the wicked ones.

Amen

Earth

The End of part 2.

tilt

up

Make relativity of my remaining space-time.

Huey E. Wolf

I'll tarry 'til

thou return

Glorify
God
within
me

edify · upbuild
w/teaching

exhortation ·
encourage

consoling ·
comforting

CYGNUS

Hans Holbein the younger

THE
COMPLETE
PARALLEL
B·I·B·L·E
with the
Apocryphal/Deuterocanonical Books

Father,
Let our work provide
spiritual meat in these
days of soup.
I humbly ask for truth,
knowledge, creativity and
power to help others in
these troubling times and
that which is coming.
In the name of your son.
Amen

in providence

Psalms 71:18

Heb.
13:6

Seek Holiness while deep within hope.

Prodigiously read the holy scriptures and commune with bYah'Yahweh Sabaoth, Jah-Jehovah of armies, Lord of hosts. Many prophets and seers called him Jah or bYah.

To survive one must conquer the wild beast and its image and number. Do not give up hope.

Faith is hope in the invisible. Trust in the Father and hope in the mercies of his Son.

Laws are engrafted in our hearts. Turn from evil, do good works, and live forever.

Death is conquered. Have no more fear of death. The devil's power is made inert.

Wisdom begins with fear of God.

Ask the Ancient of Days for more wisdom. He gives liberally to whosoever has faith in him.

Without doubt their kingdom is coming. Angelic war is coming. Spiritual war will be waged.

I am a stranger within this world. Life from the innumerable. My intact reality holds firm.

Verity bound by absolute truth. True knowledge, modicum of creativity forged into power.

Keep your conscience clean. Space/time in general relativity have never been more important.

Always help others while tarrying in prudence. Look for good and see it.

Everyone will be tempted. Resist Satan, his gods and demons, and they will flee from you.

God tests no person. Enticements from every kind of lust come from humans' own nature.

Sin brings death. The wages of sin is death—Sheol, Hades (grave or pit), Gehenna (a place of continual burning rubbish). Death is infinite for the majority. Death until the first resurrection for the faithful ones and then again until at last, resurrection. Then only life everlasting.

Suffer in this system of order for uprightness and for Father or Son to gain everlasting life.

Always be discreet and upright.

Give humility and honor to the authorities, but obey God rather than men. The choice is clear.

Babylon is the empire of all false religions. The world will be destroyed by the wild beasts.

Our God has exercised his right to rule. Merciful, just, and impartial is our coming judge.

Manifestation of the sons of God will arrive in northern Turkey. The two witnesses Jerusalem.

Do thy will until the end of man's wicked system of order.

A new beginning, much better re-creation, at The End.

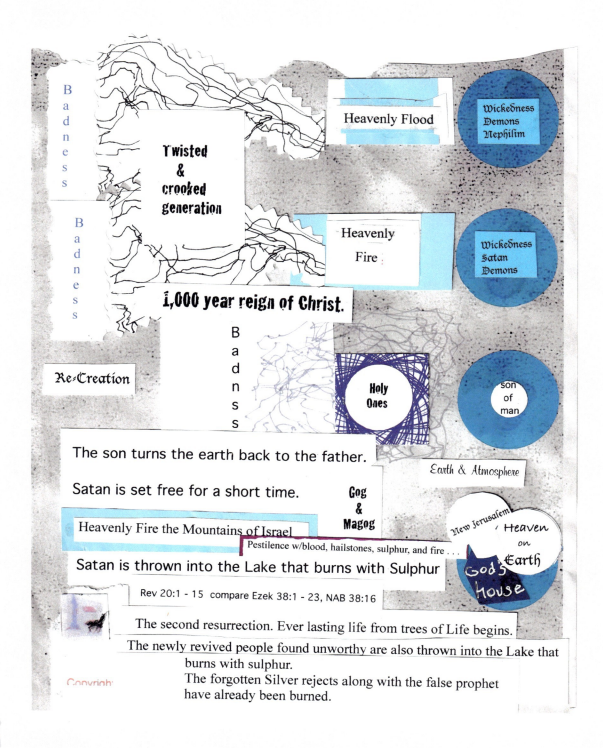

Badness

Badness

Badness

B
a
d
n
s
s

Twisted & crooked generation

Heavenly Flood

Wickedness
Demons
Nephilim

Heavenly Fire

Wickedness
Satan
Demons

1,000 year reign of Christ.

Re-Creation

Holy Ones

son of man

The son turns the earth back to the father.

Satan is set free for a short time.

Earth & Atmosphere

Gog & Magog

Heavenly Fire the Mountains of Israel

Pestilence w/blood, hailstones, sulphur, and fire . . .

New Jerusalem

Heaven on Earth

God's House

Satan is thrown into the Lake that burns with Sulphur

Rev 20:1 - 15 compare Ezek 38:1 - 23, NAB 38:16

The second resurrection. Ever lasting life from trees of Life begins.

The newly revived people found unworthy are also thrown into the Lake that burns with sulphur.
The forgotten Silver rejects along with the false prophet have already been burned.

Those beheaded for witnessing to Jesus Christ and for speaking of God.

Revelation 20:4

1st Resurrection

7

At the sounding of this Trumpeter: "Sovereignty over the world has passed to our Lord God and his Christ, and he shall reign for ever!
—Revelation 11:15

Draft